A Full Life

A Full Life

Selected Poetry of Joseph A. Cohen

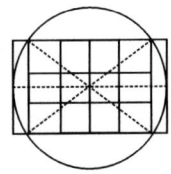

Khoni Bindery

Lowell, Massachusetts

©2005 by Joseph A. Cohen
Printed in the U.S.A.

All photographs by Joseph A. Cohen, with the following exceptions: back cover photo by Beth Cohen, photos of Bahia and Aaron Cohen by Ralph Cohen, photo of Joe in Anzio by unknown photographer.

Contact information for Joseph A. Cohen:
JCohen3041@aol.com

Khoni Bindery
Lowell, Massachusetts
KhoniBindery@aol.com

To my Sonia, my lover of 64 years

ACKNOWLEDGEMENTS

To the two who encouraged me and
taught me to use words to express how I feel
about the world around me:

SUSAN ASTOR, a published poet, teacher, and
author of several poetry books,
the latest being <u>Spider Lies</u>

KENT OZAROW, my first teacher,
a brilliant poet and a prize-winning artist

My heartfelt thanks to my daughter BETH, who
inspired me to put this book together and
who helped me every step of the way

My deep gratitude to JOE DARENSBOURG,
without whose help this book never
would have been published

I am deeply grateful for the technical and artistic
contributions of DEMETRI TASHIE

TABLE OF CONTENTS

INTRODUCTION by SUSAN ASTOR   13

1. JEWELS

My Sonia	18
She Plays Like An Angel	21
Play On	22
Christina's Trees	23
How Lovely Is Our Dwelling Place	24

2. MOSAIC OF THEIR FANTASY

Dear Ralph	27
Women Visit Arabic Style	28
Waiting	29
Café Paradiso	30
The Feast	31
Fado	32
A Room In Rome	33
The Plague	34
Buzz Bomb Christmas	35
Mosaic Of Their Fantasy	36
The Shamosh	39
On Anzio	40
Return To Anzio	43
South To North Africa	44
The Latest Loss	46
Liege Revisited	47

3. AT THE TOUCH OF LOVE

I Promised To Write	51
Sundays Together	52
The Moment	53
Another Valentine's Day, Sonia	54
Anyone For MRI	55
She Speaks	56
She Walks	57
Empty	58
"At The Touch Of Love..."	59
Sixty-third Anniversary	60

4. SUNDAYS MY FATHER ROSE EARLY

Sundays My Father Rose Early	62
My Mother Lives On	64
When Spring Arrived She Left Us	65
Andrew	66
Beth	68
Fathers and Sons	70
Lauren's Return	73
Dear Stephanie	74
The Life And Times Of Chad	75
The Birth	76
Chaya	77
Mom	78
Ancestry	80

5. MY LIFE - MY DREAMS

My First Book	83
The House I Lived In	84
My Balvenie Bottle	86
A Rebel	87
All Mine	88
Strawberry Cone	89
My Time, My Own	90
Young In Brooklyn	91
Wood To Live By	92
My Pen	94

6. MUSIC AND DANCE

Concert In The Woods	97
The Dance	98
Music In The Morning	99
The Sun Begins To Set	100
Stars Of Memorial Field	101
Our Tree	102
Musique De Chambre	103
Howling To Beethoven	104

Introduction

A Full Life is a fitting title for a book so heaped with the wonder of memories, so warm with the energy of experience. For Joseph Cohen, the world is a rich place, laden with the sensual delights of love, of nature, of art, of music. He enjoys leading us along the winding paths of his life—through a childhood imbedded in the tightly-knit Syrian Jewish community, through a rebellious adolescence and activist early adulthood, through amazing and enduring love of his wife, Sonia, through wartime, through travel, through parenthood and grand-parenthood, through the treacherous and oddly fulfilling path of aging.

Although not confessional in nature, the poems of *A Full Life* tell us a great deal about the author. Early on, we become aware of the immense joy Cohen has always taken in the beauties of nature, as in the delicate poem, "Christina's Trees," where clear admiration is shown for a woman who values trees as beings in their own right. In this poem, and in many others, we also realize Cohen's appreciation of human beings—their talents, their foibles, their sufferings. Whether he is describing his friend ("Dear Ralph") or the blind Portuguese street musician ("Fado"), the custodian at his early synagogue ("The Shamosh"), or the Algerian orphans he photographed ("Mosaic of Their Fantasy"), the poet's words are full of compassion and respect for his subjects.

Although Cohen spent years building a successful table linen business, his heart has clearly always been in the arts. With his wife, a gifted composer and pianist, he shares an adoration of music which inspires them both and has clearly inspired their daughter, Beth, to become world-renowned in the field. One whole chapter of *A Full Life* is devoted to Music and Dance.

All kinds of art inform Cohen's world. His wife is an accomplished painter as well as musician; he himself is a photographer and a photography teacher as well as a poet. Cohen's two art forms overlap as he frames his poetic subjects as carefully as his photographic ones, making each a small gem. Whether he is focusing on the plague of locusts that descended on him in North Africa, or his own "Dear Sonia" composing and playing piano with one hand after her stroke, he has the vision to see what's important in the picture and the skill to share its particulars with his readers. He brings alive everything he touches — the French countryside of "warm baguettes with farm fresh butter," Yassir, the Algerian urchin, "his bare chest aquiver with pride."

Beyond all other aspects of Cohen's tale, *A Full Life* is very much a love story, replete with details of early meetings, savored moments of intimacy, shared suffering, letters written to his beloved daily throughout the poet's years in the service, "the first...written on a ship pointed east, the last on one headed west." The depth of love between the author and his wife is palpable throughout.

There is a redemptive quality to this collection. The poet perpetually moves away from misery and toward creativity. It is apparent that Cohen took his mother's early admonition to "Be happy" seriously. In "My Mother Lives On" and in "Mom," he deals with his mother's bravado and bossiness with affectionate humor, but it is clear to the reader that he has heeded her reminder to find joy wherever possible. Even at its most painful moments, this book has an undertone of exuberance. Like his wife, even after her devastating stroke, Cohen has "a thirst for life." The strength of his poems lies in the power of the written word to re-create. His poetry revitalizes the past and relishes the future.

He makes art of war and illness as easily as he does of delightful children and delicious meals. His ability to manufacture good times in the midst of pain is beautifully illustrated in "Buzz Bomb Christmas," where the author and his friend, Madame Nys, arrange a quick Christmas celebration in war-torn Belgium, complete with turkey, cognac and small gifts. Everyone -- soldiers, neighbors, children -- enjoys the feast until "Like chaperones at a prom" the hosts "sound taps". It is impossible not to feel Cohen's pleasure at providing pleasure, impossible not to admire his refusal to forsake a celebration simply because there is a war on.

In the pages of *A Full Life*, we find heartwarming portraits, humorous anecdotes, almost unbearably tender love poems, poignant recollections of pain and of devotion, and always, beneath it all, music, keeping the beat. Reading this collection is like listening to many strands of music woven together into a remarkable whole – piano sonatas, ethnic folk tunes, delicate string quartets. The reader cannot help but be entranced.

Susan Astor
Poet and Poetry Consultant for the
Long Island Public Schools
February 2005

JEWELS

My Sonia

To see her is to behold a flower in bloom.
Radiating, glowing with charm and beauty,
her smile reflects the song of a sunlit rose garden.

Music has nurtured her being
from early childhood. Now still composing,
teaching and playing piano with one
hand, her quiet hours are spent listening
to the classics as she did when she was young.

Her eyes reveal all that she is.
A serene smile upon awakening,
a gleam at breakfast time,
a flash of energy as she
speaks by phone to friends,
her solid determination when
doing endless post-stroke exercises

Her home mirrors her taste in art whether
paintings, sculptures or exotic vases.
Surely, this sustains her will to live.
On awakening, the blinds are flung open to sunshine
and a view of tall trees shading a lush lawn.
Schumann's "Davidsbunder Tanze"
pours forth to give harmony to the sunrise.

She has shown that health problems need
not be the end, but rather the start
of a new and still creative life.
With years to go, her current birthday reveals
that growing old does not always
dull the spirit, the thirst for the good life.

She Plays Like an Angel

A radiant smile adds a glow
to the music she plays.
Her soul pulsates to the
beat of the *derbeka,* the haunting
rhythms of Sufi chants and the wild tempos of
Greek island music.

Poised and confident she plays
many bowed instruments. She
brings to life music in danger
of being buried by the roars of pop music.

She sleeps well, this princess
of world music. Like an ethnomusicologist
she performs music of past eras,
so authentic, so rich.

Like a bird she flies
from coast to coast, continent
to continent, playing exotic music.

She visits foreign lands to study
with master musicians
and to unearth hidden treasures.

For this, the folks of Turkey, Greece
and Egypt weave for her a tiara
seen only on brows of queens.

Play On

Smelling of Sloan's liniment or oil of wintergreen
four of us wobble onto the court.
Limbs wrapped in ace bandages,
bald pates bound by headbands,
the warm-up commences.

Clay-soiled sneakers combine
with once-white shorts and shirts
to complete the uniform.

Stale banter bounces back and forth.
When balls are missed, a taunt rings out,
"You would have reached it last year."

Once a tendon in my calf snapped
and I fell to the ground.
One of my partners suggested a cold compress.
Another suggested his housekeeper's
remedy, a hot compress.
A third brought a substitute player and
waited for me to disappear from the court.

Time is often called and swigging
cold water from plastic bottles takes place.
At this level of tennis,
high lobs are common as are chops and slices.
One good stroke erases the memory of many errors.

Remembering the score is not easy,
although we recall matches of fifty years ago.
At game's end, it is not important
who won, who lost, who cares.

Christina's Trees

She visits a piano teachers' meeting,
petite, gray hair framing a lively face
with radiant eyes.

The lecture on teaching jazz
to young students interests her
but does not fit.
Back in Shanghai, it was not like this.

In California, where she lives,
fig, persimmon and loquat trees
fill her garden. She greets them
when she is alone.
Speaking to trees is a private matter.
In all weather she consults them,
treasuring her bond with her special friends.

In the rain she sits under a gracious one,
giving thanks for shelter. When the sun
is relentless, it is her joy to sit
in the shade of another.
When the wind blows,
she listens to the music whistling
through the leaves and branches.

Before turning in, she whispers to them,
bidding them to stop swaying
in the wind, to go to sleep.
Early in the morning, she cuts through
fog and mist to greet her children of nature,
fondling branches as if to awaken them.

How Lovely is Our Dwelling Place

Standing barefoot on newly cut grass,
I breathe in the warmth of mothering earth.
The world within my garden walls
is filled with peaceful wonders.

Stately trees sway gently by day
yet whip wildly before evening storms.
In time of frost and cold
their bare limbs bend and crack.

How true and natural go the seasons;
rain and sunshine thaw out
life in the garden.
Caressing winds revive the greenery.
Showers nourish and feed
life within the soil.

With spring flourishing,
flowers unfold and
birds in the trees
sing out songs of life.

MOSAIC OF THEIR FANTASY

Dear Ralph

Plain face highlighted by a prominent nose,
his felt hat rumpled, weather-stained,
wearing a wrinkled gray suit, that was Ralph.

Huddled in overcoats of a winter's evening,
we stood around a Victrola
listening to records dear to him.
Midway through a Schwartzkopf rendition
of "Jesu Joy of Man's Desiring," he stopped
to re-sharpen the cactus needle.

To lift our tastes, he started by
feeding us late Beethoven Quartets.
The great Passions, Masses, Mozart operas
and German Lieder advanced our enlightenment.

Attending Shakespeare plays was not enough.
The master held readings from Hamlet, Macbeth
and Richard the Third after each performance.

Following him to parades protesting the
rise of fascism, we matured politically.
Soon, we all left to fight "the good
fight" in World War II.

I miss his wide-lipped smile, his
railing at trash in music and books,
the look of rapture on his face
while swaying to an aria from a Bach Cantata.

Raising my face to the high heavens,
I cry out to thank him for
showing me the better life.

Women Visit Arabic Style

Proper inquiries as to health and family
open this social event.
Her smile reserved for this visit,
her eyes glisten while her mind
lists the delicacies to be served.

Sugar-coated almonds (*mlabas*), rosewater
pudding (*almacia*) are the starters while young
girls go to the kitchen for other sweets.

Home-baked pastries made with filo dough
spread on silver platters that
reflect the late afternoon sunlight.

A sigh about the state of the world
is offered and all agree that
it is the will of God (*fee eed Allah*).

Before it is time to go
Turkish coffee is served
from a dainty polished brass pot.
With dignity and formal demeanor
the sighing continues until guests
make ready to leave gracefully.

Waiting

Each morning on the corner of
Nirvana and Beach where two schools meet,
he stands motionless like Rodin's
"Burgers of Calais,"
staring ahead, generating no tension.

Swarthy, white-haired,
he could be newly arrived
from Iran, once called Persia.

Does he dwell on seven or eight
decades of living,
on friends no longer alive?
Does he recollect passions of work and play?

Now each day seems the same,
no matter that streams
of lively students go up and down
the hill in both directions.

Why does he stand in this spot each day
under the elm tree,
leaning on his gnarled wooden cane?
Has his inner fire burnt out?

Café Paradiso

A winding road leading up from the piazza
to the Natural Arch is lined
with flowers, white cottages
and views reserved for God and angels.

Suddenly, at the peak
we see the Café Paradiso -- a vision
guarding the Bay Of Naples.

Atop the Isle of Capri, we meet
Rudolfo running the cafe with his lady friend.
There we dine on simple food and wine
at a table higher than the rest.

Bathed by Italian sunlight,
brushed by scented sea breezes,
we are intoxicated by his hi-fi in the sky
with music we love.

Each year when we return to this
enchanted scene, Rudolfo has a
new lady friend to wait on tables.

The Feast

Before leaving France, an invitation
to visit a friend in Burgundy
sparks our fantasy holiday.
Driving to Dijon from Paris,
quaint villages, farms, rivers
adorn the countryside.

Alighting from the car we search
for the provincial farmhouse,
slogging through hay and manure,
while greeting barnyard animals.
We pound on an old barn door and
are embraced by our Parisian friend Marie
and her Bolivian artist husband.

We are surprised as we enter to see
bright white walls, gleaming
varnished wood floors.
Music from a powerful hi-fi
echoes loud and clear with
a Beethoven symphony.

More friends pile in with greetings
ringing out in French, English and Arabic.
Soon, wines red and white begin to flow
like a river stream.
We hail the barbequed lamb on a spit,
country soups, delicious vegetables,
warm baguettes with fresh farm butter.

Humorous stories and songs of each culture
are delivered between toasts.
Heaps of pastries and fruits
wait to sweeten the occasion.

After six hours of gourmet food,
drink and pleasure,
it is time for fond adieus and warm hugs.

Fado

Late one Christmas eve, Lisbon's
glittery shops are bustling.
An old woman stands on a corner
under an old-fashioned street lamp.

Blind, a street musician, head held high,
her face shines as
she sings Fado, the music of Portugal.
With a clear and plaintive voice,
she sings songs of love,
sorrows, and the joys of living.

The next night
we seek her out by
combing each street in a pattern.
Unable to find her or her music,
we inquire of a newsboy.
"Amalia is gravely ill" he replied.

My wife and daughter are saddened.
For me, the night turns
colder and darker.

A Room in Rome

Early in June 1945, our armies
smashed out of the Anzio beachhead.
Fatigued and battle worn, we marched
into the Holy City in triumph.

Good fortune put me alongside my brother Ezra's outfit.
Our meeting took place on one of the
Seven Hills overlooking the Tiber.
We were at a loss for a night's lodging,
since hotels were off-limits to soldiers.

Wandering about the Piazza Navone,
we hit upon a dramatic first.
"Women of the Night" were plentiful,
so why not find one and pay
to stay in her bedroom
instead of buying her services?

Striking the deal was easy, but what
could she think of these "crazy Americans"
who suggested that this night
she sleep with her mother?

The Plague

Like the tribes of Israel crossing the desert,
I work in the sun in North Africa,
baking on a sand dune.
Coming from the south,
a black cloud approaches.
It billows, travels speedily, hugging the earth.

*Is this a biblical tableau
unfolding like a nightmare?*

Within minutes it envelops me
and everything about me.
Droning, whistling and buzzing,
millions of locusts eat anything edible.
They shield the earth from the sun
much like an eclipse.

As children in Brooklyn, we caught
innocent grasshoppers in empty lots.
But these were larger, relentlessly driven
by an invisible energy.

Soon, darkness turns into light.
The deluge rises, heads north.
Dazed, I return to my tasks
working in a staging area,
waiting for orders to go to the front.

Quiet falls upon the land,
nothing left but metal and wood.

Buzz Bomb Christmas

It approaches, circles, and when fuel runs out,
smashes into the earth, exploding violently.
Another V1 bomb sends its murderous message.
We comfort neighbors and curse
the winter storm that grounds our planes.

Madame Nys, our wartime hostess, invites us
to set up our cannon and tent in her garden,
as she rushes to prepare apple pie and chicory coffee
for Anti-Aircraft Gun Section #5.

How can we greet the season amidst
snow, sleet, sirens and the stench of exploding gunpowder?
The good Madame and I turn from the roaring skies
with an inspiration for a real Christmas Eve party,
a feast with music and dancing to celebrate.

Presents are army-issue towels for the women,
candy for the kids, smokes for the men --
all wrapped in tissue and ribbons
rescued from gift parcels from home.

Warmed by cognac, G.I. roast turkey, trimmings with
Belgian frittes, we long for home. This is the closest
we can be to family, friends, and the yuletide spirit.
Music of another stripe howls in the air as buzz bombs
crowd the skies above us. A parade
of singing women and children rush to
basement shelters while men follow exhaust flames
of the bomb in the sky and pray that the fuel supply
will take it further away.

Soon children's heads begin to nod, while drink
mellows the men of the 451st AAA battalion.
Like chaperones at a prom,
Madame Nys and I sound taps.

Mosaic Of their Fantasy

In the village square of Orange,
near Avignon, Algerian urchins
play and sing at sunset.
Addressing them in Arabic,
I gather them about me.

Roman ruins as a background,
the light clear and warm,
the stage is set for the tableaux.
How best to capture the colors
and seasoning of their young lives through my lens?

With a smile, I appoint Nazira the leader
and ask her to direct her
playmates to play their roles
for my camera.
She takes easily to the part of a queen
tending to her minions.

Lateefa does her
scarf dance with grace.
Joining in the fun, Karim stands
proudly, ready to take on the world.
Adela dances as if she
were performing on the banks
of the Nile.

Little Fuad, with pants dragging,
peers through tin-rimmed glasses
at all the funny capers.
Yassir waves to his unseen audience,
his bare chest aquiver with pride.

The Shamosh

Semah the caretaker sports a black bowler
perched jauntily on his head.
He is slight and dressed in
black wrinkled clothes.

Back then he called door to door
to announce in formal tones,
weddings, births and deaths.

I still picture his lean face,
sparked by clear, bright eyes
and a quizzical smile.
Chaplinesque in his strut,
blessed with sharp humor,
he is unforgettable.

Visiting the *shul* of my father,
I enter a small lobby still bathed with the
aroma of the rosewater that Semah used to pour
into the hands of departing worshippers.

His presence still hovers in the
old Syrian Jewish Synagogue of Brooklyn.

On Anzio

White vapors from smoke pots
hung over the beachhead.
Walking through fog layers
added surrealism to the battle scene.
Guns boomed, planes bombed
while cattle grazed serenely.

War co-existed with pastoral calm.
Magically, the stars and sometimes
the moon melted the white blanket at night.

One shell-shattering night,
I was awakened
by a frightened Giuseppe, a farmer
whose land we camped on.
A wartime script came to life as
G.I.s from another outfit were trying to
violate his wife Maria and two daughters.

Here was a different enemy.
Sounding a "Red Alert" which
roused the gun crew,
we ran, with rifles ready,
to the thatched hut of our host.
In his southern drawl, Sgt. Dolan
warned the drunken hooligans
to leave or have their knees shot off.

As they staggered away sullenly,
happier sounds stirred up the night.
With a grateful heart, the farmer
broke open a cask of red wine.
The boys of Battery A sang oldies
in unison, while his women
sang Italian folk songs in harmony.

Return to Anzio

So easy to remember…
I hear guns, bombs exploding,
the sounds of war.
I see smoke-pot fog
shielding us from enemy guns
trained on our tiny beachhead.

Forty years later, I return to Anzio
looking for a covered foxhole,
my home for four months.
I seek Guiseppe, our neighboring farmer,
who would not be evacuated from his
land, no matter what the danger.

Where is the pine forest that
granted shade, safety, moments of relief?
My eyes seek the ammo dump
that we guarded from dive bombers
with anti-aircraft cannons.

Country paths have been replaced
by wide, well-paved roads
spotted with billboards,
screaming to sell wine, bikinis, biscotti.

Neon lights that blind us
spell out McDonald's, cinemas, gas stations.
High-rise apartments, smoke-spewing factories
replace shell-pocked fields of green.

The historic Anzio battlefield
I lived on for four months
now resembles a bland town
in Middle America.

South to North Africa

After eighteen stormy days at sea,
Casablanca's warmth permeated
my eager but seasick body.

Exotic scents of orange trees and
rosewater pastries flavored the air.
Street-wise kids swarmed
around, offering to bring us coffee or girls,
asking for cigarettes or bonbons
in exchange.

Drawing myself up with the
dignity of an Imam, I chanted
in Arabic that they brought
shame on themselves,
with such words and actions.
Silently, they bent their heads
in disgrace.

With a dark mood hanging heavily,
a newcomer ran to me with
the usual cries reserved for
the foreign men in khaki.
The leader of the dock urchins
smacked him a powerful blow, saying,
"Be quiet, we do not beg from one of us."

Clearing a manure-soaked pasture,
we set up tents, preparing to stay.
Blue-eyed, ragged, Mustapha sat
by my pup tent smiling radiantly.
He adopted this Arabic-speaking American,
offering always to be of help.

When not running errands,
he was a fixture in front
of my canvas home in the field.
Of a Sunday, my little Moroccan friend
and I went to dine on the town.

French colonialism turned ugly
when refusing to serve an Arab child.
Naturally, we walked out until he said,
"Yousef, I am hungry."
We compromised and ate in the kitchen
where Arab waiters fed him a king's feast.

Soon, orders had us preparing to leave
by convoy through the Atlas Mountains
to invade Italy from Algiers.

Early one morning, drivers were gunning
engines, girlfriends waved goodbye to soldier lovers
while Mustapha stood by me,
with tears streaking down
his unwashed face, crying "*Allah Maahak ya Yousef*",
May God be with you, oh Joseph.

For me it was a tender moment
in the war. For him, a role model
and father figure was lost.
Sadly, he would return to the streets.

The Latest Loss

A funeral bids farewell to one we loved,
while generating rivers of memories.
At synagogue we shiver at the
frequency of such traumas these days.

The old neighborhood no longer is
what it was seventy years ago.
Stores I used to pass going to school
now have window signs
flashing alien words - -
*computers, videos, organic foods,
cell phones, beepers.*

My first school, P.S. 205, standing
across the street, remains unchanged.
Even the schoolyard fence still has a
hole for kids to sneak in
to play baseball on weekends.

Small houses surround the first synagogue
built by my people newly arrived from Aleppo.
They still stand, revived by countless coats of paint.

The orthodox service is the same,
unchanged throughout the years.
Finally the plain pine box coffin
leaves between the ancient doors.
I bid farewell as pallbearers
place it in the hearse,
one less of us to go on.

Liege Revisited

Her blue eyes, still sparkling,
brim with a flood of tears
as we meet again.
Her face even more lined
with soft wrinkles,
she hugs me as she cries out
to my wife, "I know you
from your picture
which he showed to everybody. "

We dine graciously with
French food and wine while
recalling the bombings, snowstorms
and showers of missiles both V1
and V2, that Christmas of 1944.

The following morning I seek
my favorite bistros, pocket parks,
and vistas overlooking the old city
with its majestic spires, noting the
changes three and a half decades later.
Nothing resembles the city I knew once,
not even the field atop
the *charbonage* (coal mine) where
we dug in our ack-ack cannon.

Bidding adieu to Madame Nys, I close
the curtains on that chapter of my life,
in which winning the war took first priority.

AT THE TOUCH OF LOVE

I Promised to Write

Waving adieu from the bus window,
I pledge to write daily.
How was I to know that daily
was to be for three whole years.

War swept me overseas
into holes of mud and clay.
Fear of the unknown unsettled
and scattered my thoughts.

Here was no spacious and gracious
desk to write on.
With only stubby pencils to use,
I wrote on scraps stained by the earth,
dyed by green grass.

The beat of thunderous gunfire
tapped a somber cadence
as words formed for the V mail.

The old world was fresh to my eyes.
Olive and fruit trees bent low
by the weight of luxuriant yields.
Farms, fences, foliage
lay in pastoral settings.

From afar, words served poorly.
Amatory moods can best be woven
by presence.
Colors and hues of dawns and sunsets
filled the pages with painterly images.
Always, intimacy and passion
were chilled by censors scanning the mail.

The first letter was written on a
ship pointed east,
the last on one headed west.

Sundays Together

When five cents buys a cup of coffee,
a nutted cream cheese sandwich
or a subway fare to the city,
a date can be an all-day lark.

We stroll through Central Park,
where trees and sunlit lawns bring
nature to young lovers in the
heart of the big city.

We visit the Frick
and drink in precious works of art.
We sit by the indoor fountain,
we hold hands, laugh.

Sated with art, we go on to Times Square
for a simple dinner spiked
with Cupid's nectar, apple juice.
Our dream day goes on
as we slip into an art cinema
to view a French masterpiece
starring Jean Gabin.

The day still young,
we stroll down Fifth Avenue
hand in hand, enter
a majestic old church for a performance
of The Messiah, continuing our courtship
on velvet-covered pews.

Back to the BMT line, where
for another nickel we ride back home.

The Moment

Spring hovers over the church.
Warm sunlight promises
freedom from the cold.

As the meeting is called to order,
she suddenly appears at the door,
walking with a hemi-walker.
Well into her stroke,
she overcomes timidity,
arriving to meet with
piano teacher colleagues.

First, a pause, here is Sonia
glowing with spirit, returning at last
to attend this monthly gathering.
Slowly they applaud, rise to greet her.
This is a moment luminous
with warmth and love.

Even after the poignant applause
dies down and the meeting resumes,
the moment still shines.

Another Valentine's Day, Sonia

From simple days of subway courtship,
to this, an era of mature and graceful passion,
we cling to priceless years of companionship
and a oneness ever so enriching.

We still enjoy inside flashes of humor
and intimate bedroom confidences.
When alone, reviewing people, places
and happenings has always
been relaxation therapy.

Though the years wind down
with depressing persistence, we plan new
projects, set new goals hopeful of completion.
Will there be time to fulfill our dreams?
Shall we look up or should we wind down?

Sonia, I rejoice to behold your battle to rise
from the wheelchair, to walk
to the piano, to play music for left hand.
This is the joy of living creatively.

We cherish our sixty years together,
hoping that this heaven on earth
will continue for many years.

Anyone For MRI?

In a cold white room
stripped of jewelry, glasses and hearing aid,
she enters the world of MRI.

She feels like Cat Woman from comics,
as he encloses her head in
a see-through plastic helmet with bars.
"Do not move or speak," he warns,
as the machine begins its orbit.
Lying there under the brain-reading tool,
she moans quietly:
"Why was I struck down by this cruel stroke?"

Still she is lucky to be able to think, speak,
to enjoy life's pleasures.
Her right side weakened, she teaches piano,
plays and composes music for the left hand.
Her powerful will to improve
surprises even herself.

All the while, music by Mozart is playing.
Before long the contraption falls silent.
Released from the cage,
she sits up, free to resume her life.

Wheeled out from under, she looks back
at this probing instrument, feeling that
part of her was left behind.

She Speaks

As the blinds sweep open and the
world of nature flashes in through the window,
she observes the sun, trees, sky, and whispers,
"How beautiful."

During a pause in her day's routine,
she asks, *"Where is the music?"*

Climbing five steps to enter the house,
she heaves a sigh upon reaching
the final step, muttering, *"Thank God."*

On leaving a concert, with glistening eyes
she says with emotion, *"I loved it, I loved it."*

Sitting at her easel painting watercolors
with her left hand for hours on end,
I look in on her only to hear her
cry out, *"Leave off, I am busy!"*

Just before falling asleep
in her seventh year of stroke,
she murmurs softly, *"Goodnight Joe,
yet another day."*

She Walks

Seniors upon awakening draw on
a hidden reserve of strength.
She calls on a monumental drive
to face the day's routine.

It hurts deeply to need
the help she requires.
She is frustrated at not being able
to get up and go.

Pre-stroke, she was never an Olympian.
Now she climbs the ladder of movement
well beyond limits of a post-eighty stroke survivor.

She uses muscles to get up,
determination to gather balance,
will to maintain poise,
eyes to survey the path to follow.

Sonia calls on all her powers
just to walk.

Empty

Shades drawn, deadening silence,
this, the lonely interior of a
sometimes lived-in house.
Loneliness hangs heavy when
a hospital stay keeps Sonia
from the home she loves.

No shuffling from room to room is heard.
No sounds of eating, drinking or music being played
fill the rooms up or down.
Doors hang with tension
awaiting her return.

Wind chimes hanging on the refrigerator door
lie limp, hoping to sing out soon.
Stairs do not creak, phones sit as if dead,
as do computer, fax and copy machine.

Soon she will march in triumphantly
to draw blinds, turn on the lights
and play grandly at the ebony Steinway.

"At the Touch of Love Everyone Becomes a Poet"
-Plato

Words fly with passion,
thoughts ring with feeling
and rise with the grace
of a quiet sunrise.

Lively tunes recite my devotion,
as visions of tenderness float by.
My heart beats in time
as embraces warm our caresses
with amorous play
and merge our mutual caring.
It is written that the Muse looks
with tenderness on poems of love.

Sixty-third Anniversary

There are no flowers.
There is no champagne.
It is difficult, this celebration.
Nurses take blood,
aides take blood pressure as
two of us are hospitalized,
she in room 818 and I in 401.

Neither seriously ill,
nor festive, nor joyful.
We phone each other often
like neighbors chatting.

As if by design, she goes home first
while I stay to be monitored
by a flock of caregivers.

I miss my wife, my books, my music,
my warm bed. I am told that
all will be well and that shortly,
we will celebrate our anniversary
belatedly and hospital-free.

SUNDAYS MY FATHER ROSE EARLY

Sundays My Father Rose Early

First he sets up the coffee ceremony with
a small brass pot, much sugar,
Turkish coffee ground feathery fine,
and a delicate porcelain cup.
The tray, beaten and hammered by
eighty years of use, is placed
near a sunny window from which
he views the world.

Resting in his worn, comfortable chair,
he downs the thick brown liquid.
Lighting an Optimo Blunt cigar,
he sips, smokes, and awakens all of
his senses after a deep sleep.

Never having been seriously ill in
eighty-eight years, he succumbs
to a cancer within thirty days.

Ball players have a saying,
"Way to go."

My Mother Lives On

No escaping her voice,
she yells at me, bends me to her will:
"Tie your laces, button your shirt,
where are you going? Come home early."

Even if I obey, more is yet to come.
A plea for more ice cream money
is answered by "Tear my flesh."

She ran her platoon of eight children tautly,
like a drill sergeant.
We were fed, dressed, scrubbed clean
with nary a missed step.

Wise though illiterate,
she kept our world in order.
It was said that with education
she would be dangerous.

Worn and in pain, she left us.
Always at family gatherings,
we toast her memory,
especially her joyful command
"Be happy."

When Spring Arrived She Left Us

Before she left us, I remembered
her with her hair done up in a bun,
smoking her *"nargeeleh,"* an Arabic water pipe.

How was a child to know that
grandma came to our house to die in peace?
Frail, fraught with pain,
her brave smile reflected dignity.

We sought our mother's embraces and attention
while she hugged her own mother.

Our total awareness was drawn
to a corner bedroom, while the family rhythm
beat to a different but sadder melody.

Was I selfish, was I wrong
to miss the happy chatter
from the round table at mealtimes?
We miss Grandma Sitt, a gentle
proud and beautiful woman.

Andrew

We named him after the hero of
an Irish film, "Man Of Aran."
Hearing his lover call to him lovingly
from a hilltop -- *Andrew* --
we could not but name him as we did.

In adolescence, Andrew sported
greasy hair, tight pants, a rebellious spirit.
Now in his early fifties,
mature with graying temples,
he shares California's love affair
with cars of every horsepower.

Dashes to auto markets in Europe
and American car shows rate high
in his schedule of appointments.
Tennis along with biking on the
Pacific Coast Highway keep
him fit and ruddy.

High on a hillside overlooking the vast Pacific
with views of sunrise, sunset,
surely he has found his Nirvana.

Beth

As a child she held my hand
swinging as we walked.
We skimmed flat rocks over water.
She read poetry to me.
Holding her half-size violin proudly,
she played music from her last lesson.

Driving her to summer music camp
was an adventure of word games,
reflections on nature and exploring
eating places to dine at
on visiting weekends.

Growing up in the sixties
she breathed in every
new freedom philosophy,
the scriptures of the day.

While finding herself, her mission
to achieve was torturous.
With inner strength she carved
her own path, flourishing
beyond hopes.

Earlier I worried if
this sweet, innocent child
would maintain it all
through passage to adulthood.

But always she remained
the essence of beauty, a gift bestowed.

Fathers and Sons

I pushed for cello,
he wanted drums.
We wanted David to be a brain surgeon,
but playing with a jazz combo
was more his thing.

My mother fretted over *my* rebellion.
Like his father, he too rebelled.
I am an agnostic, he chose to
become a Buddhist.

To broaden his world, he was
signed up for Little League baseball.
Watching him growl and spit like a veteran
after his best friend slammed a line drive off his pitch
was to see him mature.
This was training for adulthood
without my loving, heavy hand.

When he was still a kid, I coached him
in ping-pong, flipping baseball cards,
and tennis, till he whipped all his pals.
I taught him speed chess
between dinner courses.

Fleeing the coop for college, he left a void.
Making a full cycle, he took every music course,
even returning to play cello.
Joining my business, training to take over
added to bonding and mutual respect.

Always we could talk no matter
the stage he was struggling in.
My son, now with a family,
living in California,
is someone I have always
been happy to know, to be close to.

Lauren's Return

Nine years of heaven steps off the jet,
ending her solo flight to "magic land."
Reality sets in instantly, thrillingly -- there is no sibling
to compete for our total attention.

Returning to her world of infancy and beyond,
she is to see old friends, teachers, and the
school that formed her ideas of life outside the home.
Reading her school books, writing intimate letters,
finishing her project on Spanish Missions
are put off for now.

Whirling through the wheel of activity,
we see the ballet, the circus, parks, museums.
She has piano lessons with grandma, attends
grandpa's photo class shoot and even models for it.
Dining in places of her choice, she jokes
and sings songs from South Pacific.
She sleeps with Pouf Pouf the Easter bunny
with the innocence of a child.

It pains us to hand her over to the airline hostess
for her second solo journey,
this time back home to California.
I miss her questions, her lively eyes,
her joyful laugh.
She will never forget this visit.
Nor will we.

Dear Stephanie

1.

"The king of English was mean to the pilagrims."
Thus did our three-year old
granddaughter lecture us.

Here was history and drama from one
who knows only good or bad.
It was simple and clear:
the budding idealist faults the monarch
while offering sympathy for his subjects.

2.

Cold fear gripped her after telling the story
of those who sailed to the New World.
Two collies were entering the room,
sniffing and licking her cousins.

Watching them roll on the floor with the elegant dogs,
Stephanie's terror soon melted.
She then found courage to fondle and pet
them boldly as if she had
never known fear.

The Life and Times of Chad

A precious, heavenly gift arrived
and dazzled all.
He was reluctant to leave the delicious
warmth of his beloved mother's body.
He resisted entering the real world
since life was so sweet
in his secret hiding place.

When only ten minutes old,
he modeled for a Polaroid shot.
At fourteen hours old he
dropped into his father's office
on the way home from the hospital.

At two weeks old, he enjoyed his first
restaurant meal served by a waitress.
With only forty-eight hours under his belt,
he mercifully slept a full night
atop Mulholland Drive.

Anyone who can accomplish so much
so early in life is bound to be
a doer, a maven, a winner!

The Birth

As the sun rises in the east,
Kevin arrives with a joyous explosion.
Below him blue Pacific waters glisten,
above him white clouds dance to the winds.

Sweet innocence greets his appearance
in this alien and imperfect world.
For all the years of his youth,
warm parental nurturing
will shield him from the
harsh and ugly.

He will learn to play ball, to run
at the crack of his bat.
He will master this era's magic --
computers, cell phone and
everything digital.

Good schooling will train him
to take his place as a bright talent.
Surely he will give back because
he is fortunate.

Chaya

I see Chaya's face in all its innocence.
A quizzical smile asking
for love, attention, warmth.
Curly locks shake like holiday bells.
Sweetness from her soft blue eyes
melts all that is prosaic in her presence.
Like an actress, she tosses her head,
reaching to grab our hearts.

Mom

Once, turning onto Orchard Street,
she plowed into a horse.
It was a huge animal that
blocked the teeming street.

This street on Sundays
was always busy.
Jewish immigrants bought and sold
at either side of pushcarts.

Mom was our family driver.
Driving with untrained flourishes,
she slowed the flow of traffic,
showing no fear or embarrassment.

I was bewildered by the dying horse,
curious crowds and the burly cop.
My mother, fluent in Arabic
but not yet in English,
did not understand his Irish brogue.
The kind of talk she knew was useful,
"buy measure of sour cream",
"get bunch of soup 'n greens".

Once when neighbors called a cop because
I hit a line drive through their window,
she said "policeman, go chase crooks,
my boy good boy."

Waiting for sanitation workers to put
the horse to sleep was terrifying.
Homeward bound, once more,
she drove slowly -- but then
she always drove slowly.

Ancestry

My father left Syria in 1911 for the West,
where he put to use the only skills that had been
available to Jews in an Arab land --
petty commerce, selling cloth to the *falaheen* (peasants)
for their *jabellia* (robes).

In Syria he often traveled with a caravan
through the country, stopping overnight at *khans* (inns).
On such a trip, his convoy was stopped
by a Turkish military unit
which isolated men from women.

Males were commanded to drop their trousers.
Those circumcised were released.
Armenians, whom the Turks were
searching for, were not.
This was one time when being Jewish saved one's life.

Some time later, he marched
over the border bridge at Laredo, Texas
to seek relatives in New York.
Here he met and married my mother Bahia.

In America, he worked at what he did best,
selling damask tablecloths.
Living amidst a colony of friends
and relatives, he absorbed the transfer
to a foreign culture without heavy trauma.
After all, this was how he and his people
had lived in Aleppo, Syria for centuries.

MY LIFE - MY DREAMS

My First Book

When I was ten, my older brother
gifted me with a fifteen-cent novel.
I fondled it, opened it, tasted of it,
closed it tenderly, and hugged it.
My first book, mine alone,
to read and re-read
with intimate pleasure.

If I still owned it,
I would place it on a special
shelf in my library of thousands.
It was the first bloom in a lifetime
of living with books, books to read,
books to grow on, books for reference,
and books for teaching.

The House I Lived In

Each dawn, Joe the furnace man came
on his bike to fire up the coal furnace,
returning at twilight to bank it.
Bare of greenery and trees,
our old house was home to eight
of us kids, two parents and assorted kin.

Stucco outside, well-worn wood inside,
with rutted bricks showing the wear
of countless shoes climbing and pounding.

A scratched, dented door
looked out on our street -- a street
that hosted many a children's game.
We played stickball,
touch tackle, ringaleevio,
and raced on roller-skates.

An alley between houses
was home to many a game of
Chinese handball against the wall.

Bedrooms for four were lit by a
bare bulb. One bathroom
was shared by all. As older siblings
moved out, young ones joyfully
welcomed more space to live.

In the off-limits living room,
an old Victrola cranked out creaky
Arabic music and overtures
played by the Rookie Police Band of Mexico.

Fun came from a tinny Atwater Kent
radio which featured Eddie Cantor,
Texaco Saturday opera broadcasts
and the Longine Symphonietta.

When company came, off with the
plastic sofa covers, out with
the sweets, fruits, followed by Turkish coffee.
Lined with lace curtains, a closed-in
porch was used as our dining room.
It housed a table so large that
those sitting on the inside had to leave
last -- there was no early escape.

My Balvenie Bottle

Squat, round and proud,
it calls out, *"drink me down."*
Golden brown with a rich glow,
it is *"only the best."*

Lovers of good scotch hear it say,
*"sip me, savor me, breathe in
the essence of the good life."*
I hold it, squeeze it,
cradle it fondly.

Surely there is magic
in this hearty drink as I taste it neat.
During cocktail hours
or sitting by a roaring fire,
shielded from winter's cold,
I like my scotch.

A Rebel

After much wheedling, a bike was ordered.
It was my first, sure to shake up a
sheltered, secure, but uneventful life.
Unmindful of limits, my pal and I
headed for the water's edge,
miles from home.

Riding along the waterfront, we followed
the curves of the coastline.
More thrilling than reading or playing
tame games was this daring ride.
The wind, the sun, the salty spray from
the lower bay -- all were exhilarating.

Disciplines, structured by a decade plus
of family rule, melted as if they never were.
Biking home through strange city streets,
charged in a first daring safari,
little did I dream of the coming storm.

Missing Hebrew school and being
late for dinner alarmed
parents, neighbors, even teachers.

Their worries mushroomed into a state of
emergency, crushing my euphoric state.
Despite the storm around me, however,
this minor rebellion felt good.

All Mine

This precious clutter is what I am.
A glass tennis ball from Tiffany's,
an abacus to calculate Chinese yuan,
a N.Y. Giants coffee mug stuffed with
pencils, pens, nail clipper,
scissors, a letter opener.

My favorite pen is nondescript,
but I panic if I cannot ferret it out when needed.
Scattered notes cover the desk unevenly,
conforming to my special filing system.

Wrinkled half-finished letters
are waiting to be posted.
Paper clips and rubber bands are easy to retrieve --
they lie everywhere with studied disorder.

Books lie this way and that.
If piled end to end, they form my totem pole.
This motley selection of curious objects
all have one thing in common: I own them.

Strawberry Cone

Stumbling over uneven sidewalk squares,
I dash towards the musty drug store.
There, I buy my prize, a nickel ice cream cone
to be savored, licked and smeared
over my 8 year old face.

Rationed to one a day, it is more precious
than marbles, tops, or roller-skate keys.
Skipping down the street,
touching each landmark,
I make my way.

Seeing the weary willow tree
that never ceases to weep,
avoiding bristling hedges that ripped my
my chin once when I skated into them,
I run as if possessed.

Passing the old house
we believe to be haunted,
twirling around the sturdy fire hydrant which
served as the center of our games,
I finger outline the gnarled elm tree
whose trunk we grasp to anchor while
playing "Johnny On A Pony 1 2 3" at dusk.

Jumping over sewer covers we
use as bases,
patting the alley wall against which
we play Chinese handball,
my journey comes to an end.

With coin in hand, held ever so tightly,
I leap to the soda fountain, to order,
to clutch my tasty treat.

My Time, My Own

It wasn't always like this,
like it is now,
with someone to care for.
Now, I clear the way
for time, space,
all that she needs.

Earlier, I used to retire to rest
any time, any place,
to seize my time, my private time.

Now the pace and shifts
in the order of time have changed.
My lover of sixty years is bound
by a stroke.

A new tempo settles in,
a rediscovery of how time is spent.
Composing music for left hand,
doing her watercolors with her left hand,
and bravely working at her therapies
fill her day, with me often at her side.

The dominant theme today is reflected
by a line from an old song,
"My time is your time."

Young in Brooklyn

It was restricting for me to be one of eight,
born to a family firmly immersed in tradition.
Orthodox strictness made me rebel.
I hid dirty magazines in the basement.
Biking off the block gave me a kick.

Ignoring the call to come in,
I stayed out until the final count.
I could not resist reading Tom Swift
thrillers under the sheets,
although mom said reading with dim lights
was bad for the eyes.

Drugs and drink were not choices
but smoking was. Despite nausea
and fear of discovery, I tried
cigarettes, to be one of the boys.

Hebrew school was a nightmare.
Grim teachers tried to inflict
prayers by rote. I cringed at my desk,
hoping not to be called on to recite.

I felt penned in as I heard my friends'
cries from the schoolyard.
On High Holy days I walked to temple,
one of the crowd. Individuals were neither
recognized nor encouraged.

Each day was the same, nothing special --
I lived a clean, healthy dull life.
Yet with family insulated
from the outside world,
curiosity still burned within me.

Wood To Live By

For as long as I can recall
I chewed on pencil ends.
Lead stained my lips
after a day at school.

In grade school I doodled,
wrote love notes, took tests on
a scratched ink-stained desk.

As a Brooklyn kid playing stickball
on narrow streets, my sawed-off
broomstick poked many a base hit
through neighbors' windows.

Our old house had creaky stairs,
shiny from wear, worn down in the middle.

Our family of eight children crowded
around a large wooden dining table.
Old with faded varnish, it bore food
and drink stains attesting to
years of happy banquets.

Our bookshelves, mellow with age,
    supported treasured books,
    never groaning or sagging,
    always dependable.

Old-styled beds had mattresses
resting on slats that always
slipped at crucial moments.
We played "jump up and down,"
    causing all to crash.

Like a sailor on a ship's deck,
I would stagger and stumble
    on the pitched floors
which warped over the years.

The woods of my life,
in all shapes and sizes, had charm,
natural odors, irreplaceable warmth.

My Pen

From the era of quills and ink wells
to the present Mont Blancs,
the pen compares well to the sword.

Despite the computer, fax and email,
wars are declared and ended,
congresses enact laws and issue proclamations,
and nations achieve statehood --
all by the stroke of a pen.

Concern with all of the above
cannot be matched by my obsessive
passion for my life's blood -- my pen.
Without it I feel nude, defenseless, vulnerable.

When asked to sign credit card vouchers
or forms thrust before me,
panic precedes depression
if my fingers cannot find it to grip and to write.

Without it, I cannot take notes,
work on a crossword puzzle,
start on a new poem or list chores
yet to be done.

With it, I have confidence, security
and a *"raison d'etre,"* borne of a simple
desire to hold the black pen with
a star-shaped white crown.

MUSIC AND DANCE

Concert in the Woods

While the birds sing, flutes trill and
cellos resound with rich timbres.
Lights flicker amidst trees almost
to the beat of the music.

A hundred strong, playing as one,
sweeten the night air and velvety lawns.
Musicians fire the glow from the softly lit stage.
A golden-voiced contralto sings
to the starlit skies above.

As final notes fade, bursts of applause
sweep the open shed again and again.
Here in the Berkshires, music played
in summer lives on through the winter.

The Dance

Fronting the elevator, a couple dances silently.
A daughter holds in her arms her stroke-ridden
father who can walk but not talk.

Beth, who has brought her violin
to play for her mother in room 107D,
grabs her instrument and thrills the dancers
with waltz melodies, Russian and Jewish.

Music vibrates with nostalgia for
old times, healthy ones.
His wife cuts in on the dance
trying to recapture pre-stroke memories.

Helicopters buzz outside the windows
as tug boats chug along the East River.
Briefly, a family forgets prison bars of ill health.

Patients, aides, and nurses
pause to watch the dance, the embrace, the closeness,
on a shiny floor fronting
the elevators of the Rusk Rehab Institute.

Music In the Morning

Blinded by a sea of silver hair
and flashes of gleaming scalps,
I realize it is special to be here.

Who but seniors have the leisure,
the freedom to attend mid-morning
concerts with childlike passion?

Who but veteran music lovers
nod heads in time to allegro tempos,
sway to ineffably moving adagios?

As we enter Lefrak Hall
on the campus of Queens College,
our faces take on
absorbed expressions.

Brought up on Depression concerts costing
very little, we became familiar with
chamber music of Beethoven, Brahms, Schubert.

Lights dim in this lovely concert hall
as young musicians walk on stage
to court an audience of grandparents.

The Sun Begins To Set

Youthful pleasures wane as hopes
for living a few more years dim.

We walk with effort, read more slowly,
fight harder to complete tasks.
Falling asleep is not easy.
Once in the bosom of slumber,
we awaken at the slightest whisper.

Around me, I see wrinkled faces,
graying hair, weary eyes that
have seen much -- so much.
I know it must come to all,
but why this one or that one,
why so soon?

New friends grow not on trees
as old ones fall.
It is hard to accept that the fallen
will never return.

Stars of Memorial Field

There was a time when grandmas
resembled Whistler's mother.
Now they don't wear corsets
or lace or crinoline dresses anymore.

Spring, summer or fall mornings
they crowd tennis courts
to smash forehand drives,
or dash to the net to slam volleys.

Back then they didn't amble towards
tennis courts. They cooked, baked, baby-sat
or attended garden club teas.
Today, foursomes run fiercely and stroke
every day the courts are dry.

Dressed in stylish shorts, or skirts
topped with colorful blouses,
they talk tennis no less than do the men.
They sweat, they brag, they play, they belong.

From adjoining courts, bones creak
as senior men serve and volley,
sharing the courts with
the *Stars of Memorial Field.*

Our Tree

For decades it bloomed for only one week.
Its pink blossoms, precursors of spring,
glowed softly while it
swayed in front of our white house.

It shed its flowers
then stood gracefully the remaining
days, weeks, months.
Floating branches welcomed visitors,
as if guarding our home from evil.

Snows tipped its proud boughs,
rain bathed it, winds blew through it.

Now worn with age,
it sags, it droops as
bulges blemish its trunk.
Gone are the gay spirits it spread to all.

Alas, our weeping cherry tree
sways no more.
In its place we plant a gawky upstart,
unaware of its proud and legendary predecessor.

Musique De Chambre

The house is plain like all the others,
resembling an English row house.
Entering, we bathe in the glow
of a musical salon.

We gather for an evening
of trios by Haydn, Beethoven and Mozart.
Greetings spill over as string players
lift instruments carefully from cases
wiping them with soft cloths.

The music is placed on stands.
The first violinist raises his bow
signaling the upbeat,
and all three join in on the downbeat.
The pianist sways as she
plunges into the early runs of
the Haydn.
From time to time they stop
to debate an interpretation of
a given passage.

After a full evening of playing,
artists deserve the next movement --
delicious food and hearty drinks.
Alba's mother opens the kitchen door,
pungent spices of southern
Italian cuisine rouse hunger buds.

At dinner the same old stories are told and retold.
This isn't Vienna, Berlin or Paris.
It is music at a home, in Brooklyn.

Howling to Beethoven

More mournful than savage
is his canine cry.
Not from danger, nor in answer
to a call from the wild,
does Bongo wail.
Like his forest kin,
he howls towards the sky.

High notes from a violin have been
known to rouse dog or wolf.
Rising stiffly, body taut,
nose pointed upward as if
to pierce the roof, he trembles.

When practice is over, the fiddle
is laid to rest in its velvet-lined case,
and our friendly house dog lopes
to his lion-like lair beneath the piano.